FAITH HEALING AND RELIGION

Faith Healing and Religion

by
G. M. MES

PHILOSOPHICAL LIBRARY
New York

Copyright © 1975, by PHILOSOPHICAL LIBRARY, INC.
15 East 40 Street, New York, N. Y. 10016
All rights reserved

Library of Congress Catalog Card No. 75-196
SBN 8022-2163-7

MANUFACTURED IN THE UNITED STATES OF AMERICA

TABLE OF CONTENTS

Foreword

I.	Faith Healing	1
II.	The Nature of "Healing"	7
III.	What Is Disease?	15
IV.	Normal or Miraculous Healing	23
V.	Faith Healing and Miracles	31
VI.	The Nature of Faith	39
VII.	The Religion of the Child	45
VIII.	The Religion of the Adolescent	53
IX.	The Religion of the Adult	59
X.	Man and the Mystery	67
XI.	Faith and Healing	75

Foreword

Faith healing contains the essence and most of the substance of religion.

It presupposes the existence of a God.

It accepts that God knows about us and is concerned about our fate and our well-being. Lastly, it takes it for granted that He can and that He does interfere in the normal pattern of cause and effect (of forces acting on matter) in order to save us from ourselves or others, or to do something for us that is *not* the inevitable and logical result of the given set of physical relationships.

On the other hand, if He does not respond to our prayers and our faith by extending His divine helping hand, there is the explanation of "punishment" or of a "testing and refining in the crucible of suffering."

All this applies as much to any mundane favours and advantages that may accrue to us because of our faith or our prayer, as it does to the specific instance of the "curing of a disease."

Faith healing is therefore an ideal subject by means of which to enter the much more general problem of the nature and meaning of religion—and the place of man in the Universe.

It has been used for that purpose in this book; as a stairway and a handrail to prevent the discussion from floating off into the maze of meaningless generalizations on preconceived, but undefined and undefinable conceptual images into which this type of argument usually runs itself to a standstill.

FAITH HEALING AND RELIGION

CHAPTER I

Faith Healing

Among the subjects on which the thinking of humanity is confused, that of our so-called "faith healing" provides probably one of the worst examples.

It is true that there have been many deeply learned and admirable books written about this problem—for problem it certainly is—but these rarely reach the layman, and he, after all, is the person most concerned with it. Furthermore, almost all of them presuppose a certain specific church dogma to be valid and demand a measure of theological training in the reader, if they are to be understood.

The subject of faith healing however, goes much deeper than dogma and it is, at the same time, essentially much more simple and straightforward than such learned and complicated discussions would have us believe.

It is also much older than any dogma, or even than Christianity itself. In fact, it antedates all forms of organised religion. From the later part of the Palaeolithic age, which occurred before the first recognisable civilisations, small figurines have been dug up that have all the characteristics of the votive offerings to be found at almost all typical healing shrines of later days.

Our thinking on this subject (if we think about it at all and do not simply take it for granted as a fact) is wooly because, in it, the concepts of the professional medical and theological "sciences" together with their "lay" (but nonetheless self-assertive) counterparts, mingle and overlap and distort each other to such an extent that nobody really knows what he is talking about—or even what he *really* believes.

Here there is something that is almost the opposite of what happened at the building of the tower of Babel. Instead of having different words for the same meanings, we have different meanings for the same words. In consequence, we do not understand each other although we speak the same language.

As a matter of fact, we do not even understand ourselves because we do not realise that the important thing about the word is not the way in which it is pronounced or written, but the *meaning* that we attach to, or associate with, it.

We take the word as the meaning and the meaning as the word, unaware that the meaning of words is by no means fixed. On the other hand, even if *our* meanings are fixed for the words that *we* use, very few of us ever take the trouble to try and define, for ourselves, what those personal meanings really are.

We are content if we can attach a certain word to an event, a relationship or a situation. Having done that, we treat the subject of the word as if it, in itself, had all the implications and secondary meanings that have associated themselves with that word in our mind.

This method generally works well in daily life, but it does not work in thinking, in trying to penetrate down to the deeper meaning of things and down to what really constitutes our life.

If we are asked what *we* mean by "faith healing," we shrug our shoulders at such enquiring after the obvious.

Faith healing is healing by faith!

It is as simple as that to us. If one has faith enough, the disease will be cured. What more can one ask?

How wrong this way of thinking is follows almost immediately when we come to realise (to mention but one of its implications) that *this* concept of faith healing implies that our "faith" must then be something that fluctuates from day to day and from subject to subject for, if "faith" can "heal," then it should in the first place have automatically prevented the disease from occurring at all!

What is implied by this attitude to faith healing is therefore that "faith" is something that one applies in the manner of a surgical dressing or dose of medicine!

The problem is, by far, not as simple as all that.

This implication was not immediately apparent because we have not bothered to separate the "faith" from behind the "prayer" that we really had in mind; the "faith" itself, from the active and directed demonstration (or even application) of it. That we have overlooked the difference between "faith," "having faith" and the "using of faith" (almost in self-defence against the dangers and disasters ordained by a malignant fate) shows clearly that we have not really thought about the matter at all.

To us faith and prayer are almost synonymous in this context and healing is no more than that a disease has "got better."

To give an answer to the question, "Is there such a thing as faith healing?" one has to take it much more seriously for, to obtain a worthwhile answer to a question—one has, at least to know what one is asking.

One can, admittedly, answer it simply by stating that, as God has been able to create the heavens and the earth, He certainly must be able to do such a simple thing as to cure a cancer or to stop a galloping consumption. Furthermore, as Jesus has said that "faith can move mountains," there is really no doubt that the final answer is "yes"—so why bother about hairsplitting definitions and things?

All this is, however, based on the assumption that we know what we are talking about while, finally, the answer is given in mere generalisations on which we do not hesitate to base explanations of individual instances.

This may be sufficient for our peace of mind but it is simply not good enough as an answer. It, for instance, does not "place" *our* faith healing in relation to the undoubted cures effected by heathen rites; by the priesthoods of other, to us "lower" or "false," religions; by such inanities as bathing in the Ganges at Benares and thousands of others like it. Nor does it differentiate *our* faith healing results from those obtained by the "magic" incantations of Swamis—and the mixture of Iguana fat and ground Rhinoceros horn used by animistic native medicine men.

The real question is not if God *can* heal disease—in response to prayer backed by faith—or prayer pure and simple—or no prayer at all.

The question is if He *does* heal—and, by implication if there is evidence for His having done so.

This question is not as easy to answer as the first, although, in actual fact, it was the real meaning of that question when we asked it.

Everything is possible to an Almighty God. That is inherent in the adjective "almighty."

What we are really asking is if He can and does heal us *within* the set of circumstances, ruled by His laws, in which He has placed us.

That this is not a mere quibble, or an unimportant distinction, emerges from the expression which one hears now and then, namely that, "Here even God cannot help anymore."

It is true enough that this is only a slightly thoughtless and blasphemous way of saying things, but it shows that we too, see ourselves as living in a pattern of laws and circumstances *within* which God can, under certain conditions, no longer help without destroying that pattern or going counter to His own laws—i.e. by performing what we call a "miracle."

There is also another background to our thinking here but that will be discussed more fittingly at a later stage of the argument.

What it is intended to stress at present is that the question, "Is there such a thing as faith healing?" really asks "Does faith healing occur within the laws of our Universe *as God has ordained it?*"—and this is a very different question from the one asked by the original words. It adds a qualifying clause which we took for granted as "being understood" but which fundamentally affects whatever answer we may find.

There are many such understood provisos and qualifications hidden in the basic question and therefore it is more rational and reasonable to, at least, begin by trying to ask ourselves what we really mean with the words we use.

And first, and most important here, is the question, "What do we mean by 'healing' in this special context?"

CHAPTER II

The Nature of "Healing"

"What do we mean by 'healing'?" This is a question that troubles neither the laymen (among whom, in this context again, one must include the Theologues and the faith healers) nor even a large part of the medical profession.

And yet it is supremely important!

"A person is sick—something is done to him—he is better," is a sequence of events that, to the unthinking, constitutes a "healing," and it seems foolish or pedantic to look for doubtful points where, manifestly, there are none. The proof of the pudding has been demonstrated in the eating thereof.

A little careful consideration will, however, soon uncover the fundamental fallacy here—the confusion between "post" and "propter," between "after" and "because of."

This is a problem that has occupied "academic" medicine, often to the (at least partial) exclusion of what, to us, are some of the more important aspects of its work.

Basically "healing" has two very different meanings:

(1) There is a disease—there is no disease—the sick person or the disease is "healed."

One could see this meaning as an intransitive verb because there has been no (identified) healer. The disease just stopped. Things just came right.

(2) There is a disease—something is done to the diseased parts or functions of the patient—there is no disease: *that what has acted on the disease* has "healed" it, and (incidentally) the patient. In this meaning the verb is definitely transitive.

The trouble with the lay concept of healing, as defined originally, is that it is difficult and often impossible to be sure which of these *two* entirely different meanings it belongs to, in any specific case that may be under consideration.

It is never self-evident (except in some of the more simple forms of surgery) if the "something" that is done to the patient is "done to the patient" or "done to the disease."

In the first case, however, the healing has the intransitive meaning, in the second, and only in the second, (where the treatment acts on the disease) is there reason to classify it under the transitive meaning which is the one we have in mind when we say that a "healing" has been "done"—that a disease has "been healed" and not just "healed" (which latter indicates a fact and not a process).

It should be clear that only if a treatment actually affects the disease can it be said that "the treatment has healed the disease" (and incidentally the patient).

If this was not so, any other event—such as the going down of the sun, the bird that flew past the window and threw a shadow on the patient's face, or the glass of water that he took before his fever suddenly came down in a "crisis" —could legitimately be said to have "cured the disease."

Here a whole collection of examples come to mind.

There was, for instance, the German professor who, on the basis of rather fanciful and slightly esoteric theorising, had invented an almost universal remedy in the form of irradiated lecithin—which he called "Omnadin."

In a lecture, he showed the temperature chart of a patient as proof of his contention that it "worked." The fever had been swinging around at the 40° Celsius mark up to the point where a small red cross showed that the injection had been given. From there it dropped almost immediately to normal and remained there. The history of the case showed that the patient was completely cured. (I do not remember of what.)

The point is, however, that a few days later the ampule of Omnadin was found, unopened, in the ward. The sister had forgotten to give it after she had already marked the injection on the chart!

In passing, it was a sign of the scientific integrity of those days that the professor, with a wry smile, told the whole thing to the class at the next lecture. He concentrated after that on a less dramatic way of "proving" the efficacy of his invention but—even if it did have any success at that time—it has, by now, completely disappeared into the limbo of lost, semi-magical cures.

Highlighting another aspect of this subject, one can mention the case, reported widely in the press a few years ago, in which an American millionaire sued a famous British Urologist and obtained thousands of pounds in damages.

The patient had gone over to England to be operated on by the "greatest Urologist" of that day for a growth in his bladder. The surgeon had opened him, found a "totally inoperable cancer" and closed him up again. The man took the verdict stoically, went home and arranged his business (probably giving away whole blocks of his investments to avoid death duties) and, having done this to his own satisfaction, composed himself for the inevitable end.

But the time limit that had been given passed and, after another year, a full examination showed no sign of the growth.

Manifestly here there had been a "miraculous" healing in the first, or intransitive, meaning of the verb *for there had been no further treatment*. The patient had had cancer and he had it no more.

The reason for this cure is admittedly still a mystery but, considering it, one realises that *if* any treatment had been given, (even a palliative one) or if prayer sessions had been instituted, we would have had another, officially recorded *and confirmed,* "miracle."

The whole controversy raged about the correctness of the original diagnosis and that could no longer be proved because no specimen had been taken—but that concerns an aspect of our question which will be discussed in another chapter.

Anyone who has lived more than a few score years can remember a series of cures that have swept across the world in his lifetime.

In this century there have been the Fletchers who chewed each bite sixty times; the Hay Diet that began as a slimming fad and ended as a cure-all; the Pondorf treatment for Tuberculosis that also ended by curing everything from chilblains to acne, to mention but a few of the more striking "successes" and—only a few years ago we had the discovery of Cortisone which cured Arthritis patients right and left and brought numerous people who had not walked for years on to their feet again. Yet, some ten years later, it had to be pronounced to be "no more effective for arthritis than a few aspirins."

One would not find it difficult to fill a whole book with an account of this kind of thing.

Turning to the more scientific side of our question, there was the case of Bleuler who was the superintendent of a large mental hospital in Germany, some forty, fifty years ago. He claimed that *all* the medication practised by the profession in his day was so much quackery. (This was before the advent of the antibiotics that *are* able to produce what would, at that time, have been considered to be true miracles.)

He therefore, in typical Prussian style, forbade all forms of medical treatment for his patients and, lo and behold, after a year or so of this, the medical statistics of his hospital were no worse—and even slightly better—than those of the preceding years or those of other similar institutions.

Inversely, one can note that the medical profession itself

admits that in a certain percentage of cases (how large, no one would dare to estimate!) the longer duration, if not actually always the disease itself, is *caused* by the medication and the treatment.

It even has a special name: "Iatrogenic conditions."

Although this may have shocked the layman somewhat, it is partly, if not largely, his own fault, for what he demands is treatment—and more treatment—especially expensive treatment that must be "good" because it is expensive. It does not matter to him if all the theory has been worked out or if the available data have been adequately assessed. He is prepared to take the chance for *he* does not have the time to wait. He is sick *now!*

It is, for instance, mostly due to this attitude of the patient that the inestimable gift of Penicillin has been wasted in a few years by splashing it about in such an uncontrolled way that the "infections" have acquired a resistance against it which, in America at least, is by now, almost complete.

To know if a treatment really *heals* a disease, there are only two ways open to science. Either one must know *exactly* what the disease is and *how* the treatment affects it—or a sufficiently large, comparative statistic material must be available about treated and untreated cases.

It is for this reason that academic medicine has taken the opposite attitude by demanding that a full diagnosis must be made before treatment is instituted—which leads to such apparently bizarre extremes as the professor who erupted into a blazing temper because a "provisional" treatment had been given and cured the patient before a full diagnosis had been arrived at!

In a way he was even right for it was now obviously impossible to know if the patient had been cured by the treatment; if he had just become better or, if he had become better *despite* the treatment. It had been a completely unscientific way of going about curing the disease!

As to the statistical method—it also has its disadvantages. Those who have read Sinclair Lewis' book "Arrowsmith" will remember how his conscience was troubled by the method of determining the efficacy of the vaccine against Yellow Fever by giving it to only half the patients. In that effort to find the truth, the controls were condemned to die as a proof of the fact that it worked in the others—if it worked at all!

These stories may have been interesting to the layman who, alas, seems to have an almost morbid interest in diseases and the problems of "doctoring"—but they were necessary to outline and define the background, and to give the reader a small insight into the real nature of the problem itself.

What he possibly has not realised is that it is into this shadow-world of fact and fancy, science and imagination, hopes and fears and blind but careful, infinitely patient probing for knowledge and information, that the "faith healer" enters with a supreme confidence which would be ridiculous if it had not been so tragically and dangerously foolish.

To him, bless his innocent soul, all *his* cases that are healed because of his (or their) faith. To doubt *that*, to him, is almost blasphemy; a doubting of the power of God to cure the sick!

For him there is no such a thing as the intransitive meaning of the word healing in relation to *his* cases or in relation to anyone who has been prayed over, or on whom the healing hand has been placed.

Not for him the need to know what exactly the *nature* of the disease happens to be. They are all "diseases" to him and his God. The people are sick, faith is applied in some way or other, the patient is better—and who would *dare* to deny that the hand of God Himself has been active there? (What he forgets here is that it is not the same if the hand of God is considered to be active *in response to*, or *at the behest of*, faith, or if it is active in the way that that same hand of God is concerned in *everything* that happens, even in that which caused the disease!)

Part of this fervour is naturally due to the satisfaction that it gives the healer to feel himself to be an instrument of God, so that in a way he is God's partner in alleviating the suffering of humanity. Consciously or unconsciously, being only human, he will tend to fight to a standstill to retain this idea, and one can forgive him, because one can understand it.

Far worse than this, however, is his abysmal ignorance about that with which he is actually dealing *and* the complete worthlessness of the *foundation* for his claims of divine *interference* in the course of the disease that has been healed.

Here the faith healing practitioner (and the Protestant Churches as a group) would do well to take a leaf out of the books of the Catholic Church for, although it publicly encourages the pilgrimages to its holy shrines, to which its members flock in their thousands, it has a very strict, private analysis of the "cures" effected there.

The pilgrimages are encouraged because they promote piety and the reality of God to the pilgrims, but over the ages, only a handful of cures have been officially declared to have been truly "miraculous," that is: due to God doing something outside of, or in spite of His own laws.

CHAPTER III

What Is Disease?

In the foregoing discussion it was not possible to come to a real insight into what "healing" means because we had not taken the elementary step of deciding what we mean by "disease"—the subject from which all our attempted definitions *had* to start.

What, actually, *do* we mean by "disease"?

It is not really a "something" that is in a sick person, although we almost automatically visualise it as such because we "have a word for it."

The concept therefore remains foggy and no thinking can produce clear answers from such ambiguous premises.

As said, disease is not a "something" that is in, or that has entered into, a sick person. It, alas, is not something that "goes away," either voluntarily or by being forced to go, when he gets better—or is "healed."

It will be found that it is exactly this idea that makes it so difficult to think of healing without a "healer." The thought that a disease that has had the ability to establish itself in a body, should leave of its own free will is not really acceptable. It would need, we think, a "something else" to *make* it go.

One can feel that this is the remains, the sediment, of the idea pervading all primitive medicine, and even the New Testament which saw all diseases (both physical and mental) as evil or malignant spirits that had to be "cast out" by magic, or any other available method, if the patient was to be cured.

Not having the information available to us, they could hardly have thought anything else and therefore the largest part of primitive medicine consists of "making it unpleasant for the invader" (without taking too much notice of the almost inevitable fact that their treatments made it just as unpleasant for the patient!)

Here there are also the purgatives and the emetics, the bloodletting, needling, leeches and "cupping"—and finally even the trephining, the making of a hole in the skull, inside which such an evil spirit might have found itself trapped and unable to come out. This latter method was already practised by stone age man.

All of these try to make a "something" come out of the body—they do not really try to "cure a disease."

The "casting out of evil spirits" idea disappeared there where civilisations developed. It remained only in relation to madmen and epileptics whose actions seemed to confirm the idea that they had been "possessed." Bloodletting lost favour in our great grandfather's day. Routine purging and the administration of emetics remained longer because they *do* have a certain beneficent effect in many of the diseases inherent in our way of life.

In the meantime, out of the magic potions and simples of the witches and, later, the herbalists, a more effective way of treating diseases by means of substances that were known to have certain definite effects developed. But, even there, magical properties and the way of seeing a disease as a "something" in the patient lingered on, as is evidenced by the cure-all nature that most of them were thought to have. They were thought to be effective "against heart, and kidney, and liver and lung diseases" no great matter what those diseases really *were*.

All this goes to demonstrate the effect of not thinking clearly and not being careful with the words one uses.

A disease is not *in* a person—and it does not go away when it gets better. It does not "go," it "stops," and even that is wrongly expressed, for it is not an "it" that can "stop"!

The real nature of diseases and healing lies in that the normal functioning of the healthy body of the patient begins to function abnormally when it gets sick and that, when it becomes well again, it resumes its normal functioning.

"Sickness" or "disease" are nounifications of an adjective —and what is more, they are negative in that they really mean: "not-healthy."

When a patient becomes better, his sickness has not gone, his "health has been restored," which may seem to be a mere playing with words but which is pre-eminently important in regard to one's attitude to disease.

One can perhaps best compare this to a motor car in which the timing has slipped. There is not a "something" in that car that makes it weak and causes it to backfire for apparently no reason at all. Its pattern of functioning is out of true and, when that has been corrected, it is not "cured" of its "malfunctioning." It simply functions normally again.

On the other hand, the fuel jet in the carburetor may become clogged up by dirt. Admittedly, *now* there is "something" in the engine that makes it function badly, but this bad functioning is due to an insufficient fuel supply and not to the bit of dirt. If the bit of dirt is removed or *if in any other way*, the fuel supply is restored (say by installing a second fuel pipe and jet) the engine will function properly again and be "healthy," despite the continued presence of the blocked jet.

Lastly, the car can be driven by a drunken driver and run all over the place except straight down the road as it should. But, if that drunken driver is given a chance to sober up, the whole combination will be as good as it ever was.

In the same way we can see, what we know as "disease," to be due to one or more of three causes disturbing the normal functioning of "health."

This normal functioning can be defined, for our purposes, as the pattern of forces and materials, the balanced action and reaction, that permits the body to do its work and that gives the awareness its sense of well-being which we find "normal" in a human being.

Any change in that pattern which, actually or potentially, wholly or partially, destroys or endangers that normal functioning is a "disease."

(The reader must have patience with this analysis for it becomes supremely important later on.)

There are, in analogy with the examples of the motor car, three principle ways in which this normal functioning can be adversely affected and, singly or (usually) in some kind of combination, be the cause of what we know as diseases.

In the first place, there is what one could call an "unbalance" between the component details of the patterns, either in the materials or the forces concerned, or in the "timing" (that is, in the promptness of the needed responses).

In the second place there are the "invasions" by other living entities. It is true that here there is a "something" in such a sick body, but these invaders *are* not the disease. They cause it in the body of which they upset the normal functioning.

In the third place there is the, only too often forgotten, mental factor.

The Romans had a saying: "Mens sana in corpore sano," i.e. a healthy mind needs (or has) a healthy body to live in.

One could as well invert this into "A healthy body needs a healthy mind to rule it," and as usual, the truth is somewhere in between. A healthy body may contain a diseased mind—a healthy mind is not sufficient to maintain a body in a healthy state if that body is abused or suffers from too aggressive an "invasion."

The brain rules the functions of the body by three methods.

Firstly by the obvious way:—the nerves that stream out from its base to every nook and cranny of the body. These nerves are concerned with getting information from the outside and the regulating of the reactions of that body to the physical condition *in that outside.*

The largest part of this is conscious, that is, the mind knows about what is happening in it, but, nevertheless, a very great part of it is sub—or unconscious—almost automatic and cybernetic in its actions.

When the biceps contracts, the muscles on the opposite side of the arm relax *exactly* the right amount. Minor harmful stimuli are reacted to in a way which stops them, even before the mind becomes aware of them and consciously institutes the appropriate reactions. There is furthermore the intricate process of balancing the body while walking and the catching of something (like a thrown match box, or a ball) of which only a part of the trajectory, at a distance, is "known." One can make the list almost as long as one likes.

The second system of control is via the sympathetic and para-sympathetic nervous systems that rules the functions of the body *itself.* It is mostly unconscious—although not wholly so, as one experiences when one has a colic or an attack of angina pectoris in which an urgent distress signal is sent up into the brain.

It functions by means of a finely adjusted balance between the two systems that counteract each other according to information picked up locally *and* the general instructions sent down from the head-office in the brain.

Among its functions are the control of skin temperature, blood pressure, local dilatation or constriction of the blood vessels according to the needs of the parts concerned or the body as a whole, the contractions and relaxations in the intestinal muscles, secretion of body fluids, control of the heart beats, and a number of other functions too numerous to mention here.

In this domain, when things go wrong, we have the symptoms of "Shock," "Asthmatic diseases," "Gripes," "Diarrhoeas," "Constipation" and similar troubles.

Lastly there is the hormonal (biochemical) control by

means of a small gland at the base of the brain; the "Pituitary" (and possibly others).

This, again, by means of an infinitely complicated and delicately balanced system of action and counteraction, rules the chemistry and the growth functions of the body (although it shares these duties to a certain extent with the sympathetic-parasympathetic system).

When things go wrong here, we have the Diseases of the ductless glands: Dwarfism, Infantilism and Gigantism, Sexual Abnormalities, Thyroid diseases and similar conditions.

Below this extensive, unimaginably complicated, and still more unimaginably finely adjusted system of government, there are the billions of body cells that have retained a certain amount of "personal existing." Each of them has an individual, inner organisation which, nowadays (with the electron microscope and the new microbiochemical methods available) is showing an almost breathtaking complexity of its own.

These are the "citizens" of our body that usually obey the "orders" from "above"—but that do not *always* do so, as is probably the case in "cancers," where they keep on growing by themselves.

All this is simple physiological fact and in no way the product of a fanciful imagination. All of it can be found in any elementary textbook on physiology and should, at least in its general outlines, be known to anyone who pretends to have the right to have opinions about "healing" and its possibilities and implications.

The point here is that, in the brain, in the central control room therefore, there is also the mind, the awareness and, although most body functions are able to look after themselves sufficiently well, the final overall pattern is in the hands of the "mind."

If that mind is uneasy, the body will take the function-pattern of a body that is in danger. Certain, at the moment, non-essential functions will be suspended, others accentuated or held in readiness for action. If the mind is at peace, with itself and the world outside, the whole pattern will function as economically as possible.

Fear, displeasure, anger and hatred, all have their effects on the normal functioning of the body, which may therefore be in a function-pattern normal for a condition that does not obtain outside, but one that is not normal for the conditions that are actually there.

It may be ready to jump or fight when there is no danger, or not ready to do so when there is. It may feel hungry and eat when it needs no food or lack appetite and starve itself when it needs it. It may sweat when it is cold and refuse to sweat when it is overheated, keep its muscles tense when it should relax in sleep or relax when it should be on its toes —all because the mind, the big boss, has got his signals mixed.

Only if one understands this can one have any idea of what disease entails and, therefore, what "healing" must be thought to *do* to "correct" it.

CHAPTER IV

Normal or Miraculous Healing

When health is restored to the body the process of healing obviously has to be different for each of the three kinds of "diseases."

What is not realised—or often forgotten—is that all three of the transitive "healings by a healer" have an intransitive counterpart: a self-healing ability that is present in the functioning of the body itself. This latter is not an active and purposeful healing *by the body*, but a simple tendency to return to normal functioning, if that is at all possible.

The ability to return to normal functioning is inherent in all living tissues. If it had not been there, life would have disappeared from the face of the earth long ago. Indeed, it is doubtful if it could ever have appeared at all!

It is a part of the cybernetic (self-correcting and adjusting) aspects of the normal pattern of life itself. Every action in it has a counteraction, every function a counter-function, which is *automatically* set into motion by the antagonist at a certain stage of its activity.

When this counteraction is not strong enough, or too slow, (or if the action itself has got completely out of hand), we have what we known as "disease."

Self-healing occurs when the counteraction manages to catch up, either because the action has slowed down of itself or because an added stimulus has boosted the counteraction into greater activity.

For this reason (before antibiotics) all effective non-surgical treatment was actually an assisting of the body to heal itself although this was not usually realised, even by the doctors who instituted it. The doctors, the medicine and the nursing did not "cure" the patient or the disease. They made it possible for the counteraction to take effect. As said, they *assisted* the body in healing *itself*.

When one realises the implications of this, the healing of the "disturbances of the pattern of functions" diseases consists of strengthening those components that are too weak and weakening those that are too strong—until the "give and take" between the opposing factors is again taking place within the normal limits laid down for it.

The healing of the "invasion" diseases—that is, the "infections"—entails a strengthening and promoting of the natural defensive measures that consist of detoxificating or neutralising the poisons produced by the invaders, fabricating poisons that will kill the invaders, the swallowing of the invaders by the self-sacrificing white cells of the blood (that usually die in the process), making the climate of their environment unhealthy or uncongenial for the invaders—and numerous other methods of which we have, even now, only a sketchy idea.

As far as the mental conditions are concerned, healing must consist in what we simply call "getting it back to a normal, well balanced, common-sense attitude to the world and to itself."

These are the *necessary* ways in which one has to visualise healing provided one does not solve the question for oneself by supposing that the slate is simply wiped clean and a normally functioning system installed in its place—which would be a "miracle," even in the case of an ordinary nose cold!

It is a typical, human, one could almost call it "parochial," thinking error to consider the sudden disappearance of a large cancer, the raising of the dead or the restoration of a hand that has been destroyed by leprosy to be a "miracle" and not to give that same name to the sudden cure of a pimple.

As a matter of fact, even the killing off of a single bacterium or the removal of a single molecule of thyroid hormone in a case of Grave's disease, *by other than the normal means,* would be as much of a miracle as any of those that Jesus did because, as He said, "Except ye see signs and wonders, ye will not believe"!

It is the essence of the concept, or meaning, of the word "miracle" that it is something that is done outside of, or against the laws that God has made inherent in this world in which we live. And this definition applies as fully to the small miracles as it does to the large, impressive ones mentioned above.

The question which we are facing at present is if God can (and does) heal us *within* the set of circumstances ruled by His laws, in which He has placed us?

No believer in an Almighty God can doubt that He *can* perform miracles if He considers that they are necessary.

In this context we therefore have to make ourselves clear on the point of: "What do we mean by the laws of God"?

Only by knowing that we can know if we are thinking about simple "healing" or about "miracles" when we think of "faith healing"—even if, *in that case,* we are also forced to see a miracle in the healing performed by a witchdoctor or a swami.

One cannot have it both ways!

After some consideration it emerges that the "laws of God," in so far as they concern the physical world, *must* be the same as the "laws of nature" as defined by Science.

The difference, to us, lies only in our human attitude to them, not in what they are, or represent.

Science sees these laws as being there, by themselves, and feels no need to refer them to a God (in Whom the individual scientist may or may not believe without it making any difference to the laws themselves).

The Church, on the other hand, feels, or knows, that it has

the quintessence of *all* Truth in its scriptural revelations. It sees the mere laws of nature as belonging to the worldly domain of the Scientists which is, at best, of only secondary importance.

If the laws of nature in building up to a conclusion, arrive at something that goes counter to what the Church reads in (or into) its scriptures, these laws are necessarily wrong because it, unknown to itself, confuses the "scriptures" with its "interpretation of the scriptures."

By doing so, both Science and the Church perpetuate and aggravate a difference that *does not exist*—and that cannot exist if the Bible is a truly inspired book!

Science merely concentrates on the laws God has ordained for His physical world. By carefully examining that world, it tries to discover how that world has been put together and how it works.

The Church, considering the physical world to be only of secondary interest and importance, is apt to draw conclusions and make pontifical statements about it on the basis of its *personal* way of understanding the words of the Bible—and without a profound conception of what it is really talking about. And, having done that, it ascribes to these personal interpretations the same absolute validity as it ascribes to the religious, metaphysical part of the whole of the "laws of God," as found in the Bible.

The unpleasant and somewhat humiliating result of this attitude has been a long series of clashes between the Church and science in which the former has always and inevitably had to give in.

When the analysis of "facts" contradicts its interpretation of scripture, the first reaction of the Church has always been to cry "Blasphemy!"—from the reaction of the Catholic Church to the "heresy" of Galileo to the vituperative rejection of Darwin's Theories by, primarily, the Protestant Churches.

Yet, in our day, the earth is no longer a flat dish resting on four pillars, the sun has silently moved into the centre of our planetary system, vaccination has become a boon to humanity and madmen no longer have a devil in them, to mention but a few of the more striking examples of ecclesiastical retreat.

The Church has even had to admit, albeit grudgingly, that there may be some truth in the Theory of Evolution and that it is possible that God has "made" man by normal means.

This continuous rear-guard action, which has prevented the Church from being, as it should have been, the leader of human thinking, is due to the fact that it has not realised one of the most important truths of this world.

It may be correct that, as it believes, we have, in the Bible, a book that God has inspired men to write for us—but we also have, in nature and the world around us, a book that He *undoubtedly* has written Himself!

It is for this simple reason that, when there is a discrepancy, it is God's *own book* that has the last word!

Essentially the trouble lies in the interpretation. There *can* be no discrepancy between what has been actually written in those two books, if the Bible has been inspired.

If the scientist interprets the book of reality in such a way that its facts tell us that Man descended from the animals, it is not enough for the Church to say, "Nonsense! The Bible says that he was 'created.' "

It will have to join issue on the way that science has done its *interpreting* of God's book and to show that the facts can mean something else—something that is in agreement with what it reads into the Bible text. It should have learned by now not to read only one book of the two with which God has provided us.

If it cannot read any other meaning into the facts of science, it must examine the validity of its *interpretation* of its own textual authorities and it can then happen that it will realise that Genesis uses the words "create" and "make" as synonyms, as Genesis 2:4 shows all too clearly: "These are the *generations* of the heavens and of the earth when they were *created*, in the day that the Lord God *made* heaven and earth."

Both the words "creating" and "making" here seem to have the same, intended, basic meaning as the first word "generating"—which is exactly what the Theory of Evolution claims that happened.

According to it, Man was "generated" out of the animal kingdom *according to the laws of God.*

One has to establish this identity of the laws of God with those of science, *and its implications,* clearly in one's mind for it is all-important in relation to the subject of "faith healing."

The laws of nature concerned in the process of healing are fairly simple.

One could define them as follows:

(i) Every physical object is where it is.
(ii) No thing can come into existence out of nothing.
(iii) No thing can vanish completely into nothing.
(iv) In moving from one place to another, a thing occupies all the intervening places.
(v) A thing only moves or stops moving, or changes its speed or direction of movement, if a definite force acts on it in a certain way.

These laws hold true, not only for "things" but for parts of things, right down to the molecules and atoms of which it consists.

Below that, at the level of the nuclear particles, this becomes more complicated as these nuclear particles can form themselves out of pure energy or be changed back into pure energy again—as the horrendous Atomic Bombs have demonstrated a score of years ago.

But that does not apply to our *ordinary* world.

These then are the simple basic laws of God within which, and in accordance with which, we must find the possibilities of "healing"—either by medicine, by treatment, or by faith. And, if we accept that, it must become immediately apparent that only *physical* forces can do this in the case of the malfunctions and the invasions.

No cell, substance, molecule or atom can be made to move or to do something, except by means of a force. And, if that force is not inherent in the pattern of living itself, it must be added—i.e. it must come from "outside." Hence there must be a "miracle"—something that happens against the laws of God.

Therefore *all* healing (that is not miraculous) must take place through the normal reactions that are at the disposal of the body, no matter if it happens in official treatment, during a heathen rite or during a Christian prayer session.

And the only place from where that can possibly be done (if not by means of directly applied human, physical means) is in the "head office," the brain where the non-physical "mind" has the ability to influence the physical pattern of the whole, either to its advantages or disadvantages.

Only the mind (conscious and sub-conscious and unconscious) can therefore "heal" in any but a miraculous way (in this context), and it is therefore this mind that must be influenced by faith, if "faith healing" is to be possible *within* the laws that God had set to rule His Universe.

CHAPTER V

Faith Healing and Miracles

Our examination of "faith healing" and its implications has now arrived at a stage where it is possible to face up to an aspect of it that has purposely been held vague, namely: the very real and most important difference between "faith healing" and a "miracle."

In most of our thinking, we tend to see these two as being almost synonymous—as they were to the apostles and the writers of the New Testament who were totally ignorant of both physiology and pathology and hence did not know what they were healing; and what that healing actually implied.

To this kind of thinking, based on external appearances alone (and without any understanding whatsoever of what is involved) there is, at most, only a difference of degree. The relatively common disease that is healed "without medicine" by faith, is a small miracle. The great miracle is, in this context the healing of a disease that we believe is to be "incurable."

What happens in both cases is essentially *the same* as far as we are concerned.

However, most of us are unable to draw a line between "curable" and "incurable" diseases, for the simple reason that we do not have the beginning of an idea of what it is all about. The *whole* process of "curing by faith," therefore, has attained (or retained) an aura of the miraculous in which the miracle is merely more or less impressive in an inverse ratio to the chances that *we* think that the disease had of being cured by itself, or by the merely "human" efforts of the medical profession.

In this way it all becomes a manifestation of an essentially identical event which, if examined, turns out to be a healing that happens due to something that is "not of this world," as a response to an expression of—or even the mere presence of—"faith."

As, to a certain limited extent, these results can also be produced by natural, worldly means, it is therefore in comparison to these "ordinary" possibilities of healing that the observer judges the magnitude of the "miracle" he sees in any individual feat of healing by faith.

In consequence the possibilities of faith healing are not determined by the "faith" in the healing power—but, ironically, by a lack of faith in the ability of the body (and mind) to heal itself! This is essentially the same thing that makes it a sine qua non that the doctor *must* write out a prescription, even if he knows that a few days in bed will do the trick. *Something* must "heal" the "disease" and, if it is not medicine or surgery, it—to the religious person who has prayed for healing—must be a "Divine Power," whoever or whatever the implied divinity that is considered to have that power may happen to be. The possibility that the body, or the mind cures itself is overlooked.

Otherwise than in the times of the apostles, we, with the knowledge provided by our instruments and the understanding provided by our science, can draw the line between the simple healing that takes place according to the laws of nature (and therefore according to the laws of God) and those that would need a "miracle" to occur—that is: a healing despite and contrary to those laws.

Admittedly, that line is not yet as sharp and well defined as one would like it to be, but, except for some borderline cases, it can be drawn with reasonable assurance.

This dividing line is the one that the Catholic Church tries to draw (consciously or unconsciously) when it attempts to sift out the true "miracles" that happen (or are thought to happen) at its shrines, from the mass of "ordinary" faith healing *that those shrines have in common with all the others mankind has ever established for that purpose.*

Recalling the relevant laws of God and nature listed in Chapter IV, one can distinguish two possible kinds of miracles or, rather, two kinds of aspects of healing that would make a mere "healing" into a "miracle."

The first would entail the sudden disappearance (not absorption) of material substance, such as tumour tissue, or noxious fluids, or individual "invaders." On the other hand there is the equally sudden appearance (not formation) of new material, such as new bone, in the sudden healing of an old fracture that has consistently refused to heal (this would also entail the disappearance and of the interposing soft tissue materials that were there before)—or hormones that no "gland" has produced—or antibodies that suddenly begin to kill off the invaders.

Any cure that has to entail either manifestly or by implication the conclusion that such an event has happened would necessitate the deduction that a "miracle" had occurred (because, in involving a "creation" or a "de-creation," it would have happened against the laws of God and nature).

The second kind of miracle is not as easy to define and substantiate as the first.

This would be one which entailed the taking effect of a "force" that had no natural explanation or cause.

Here it is all too easy to accept that a certain force was not "normally" explainable, or, on the other hand, that "in some still unknown way" it was after all "natural." The choice is up to those who (for reasons of their own) either want, or do not want, to believe in miracles.

It is not easy to visualise a force and therefore difficult to have a clear mental image of what has happened, or must have happened, to effect the cure.

Here let us imagine a rifle and a target, both immovably fixed in such a way that the straight line down the barrel of the rifle, if prolonged, passes through the centre of the target. If the trigger is pulled, the bullet will inevitably and according to the laws of nature, score a bull's eye every time (if the target is not too far away from the muzzle of the rifle).

It is not too difficult to accept that God, *without performing* a miracle, could deflect that bullet to one side by "influencing" its flight pattern—and make it score no more than an "inner."

But this is a thinking error.

To have done so, He would still have had to exert a real and physical force on that bullet—and it does not help to try and avoid the issue by saying that He could have done this by causing a strong wind to blow across the rifle range. That would merely place the "miracle" somewhere else—namely in the forces that would have had to be set into motion to produce that wind!

As the work of science shows us with almost infinite, meticulous exactitude, force is an expression of the effect of energy. And energy, like matter, cannot be destroyed or created *within* the laws of the universe in which God has ordained that we should live.

It follows therefore that anything that does not happen exactly according to the configuration of the pattern of energy distribution in *any* situation, is as much a "miracle" as one in which there is the appearance or disappearance of matter. The difference is merely *in* us, in that we can see matter but cannot be aware of energy in any other way than by its effects

God, therefore, *cannot* influence the physical world in any way without superseding or nullifying the laws that He has laid down for it, and it is a symptom of a simple, unsophisticated (not to call it, essentially "pagan") world image to see God as influencing events by means other than the forces and energies that He has made inherent in the world *in the beginning*. Having once made it, He cannot influence it otherwise than by interfering with the pattern of His own creation. If we like to see it in that way or not, *all* interfering and influencing by God must have the essential qualities of a "miracle."

Ordinary healing, however, does not need His interference in this sense at all, not even in the mind of the person who is being healed.

As explained earlier on, in most cases all that is necessary is a calming down and a bringing back to a more balanced state of mind—and *that* is what faith does—no matter in what that faith has been placed. And this holds true even where the object of that faith is a mere figment of the imagination.

By its very nature faith is something that is greater and more powerful than we are, faith in something that is thought to be able to control the events in the often inimical world of reality, leads to a placing of one's fears and worries about the future in its care—with a consequent relaxation of the inner, personal tensions. In realising that there is nothing one can do about it; in giving the problems of the situation into the care of something greater than oneself and in trusting that He, or She or It will hold us safe, the inner person stops interfering with the functions of his own body, stops pulling levers that should not be pulled and pushing buttons that set things in motion at the wrong time.

Therefore all faiths can heal no matter what the benevolent "power" is in which one has put one's trust.

A fact, the importance of which is usually overlooked here, is that there are many cases in which the use of some superstitious formula or device, such as wearing a bangle of dried seaweed, or the insertion of copper-lined inlays in the shoes, will effect a cure despite the fact that the experimenter is genuinely sceptical. *This is not because he has a subconscious faith in them* (as it is usually explained) but because, in observing the effects of his own "foolishness," he has *temporarily* shelved his tensions and worries! In, as he thinks, giving the "superstitious nonsense" a chance, he is giving his own inner self a chance to get back to normal—which it promptly does with results that are often extremely surprising to the experimenter, and another "proof" of the efficacy of the cure to the true believers!

Neither the faith, nor that which is the object of that faith, "heals" the disease. Neither the simples of the witchdoctor, nor Amenophis, nor Tau—nor God, effects a cure in ordinary faith healing. The body will do that, just as it did it in the case of the Greek doctors and the good G.P. of our youth.

The faith stops what *causes* the illness, it does not cure the illness.

And the important point here is that, if the illness is of such a nature that the body *cannot* cure itself (anymore)—then neither can faith, however strong it may be—*unless a miracle takes place.*

From this it follows that, if we ask God anything, we must not ask to be cured *because we have faith*—we must pray for faith enough in Him to stop us from being afraid. It is faith and trust in Him that we lack when we "pray to be cured"—faith and trust, both in Him and (if we neglect to use them) in the medicines and treatments that He has permitted us to discover as being able to help our body to cure itself.

(In the latter case we are like a man who prays to God to stop the rain that is making him wet and uncomfortable, instead of moving in under a nearby roof.)

There is a certain amount of truth in the primitive and essentially heathen idea that disease is a "punishment" but it is not a punishment in the sense that we have sinned and that His vengeance has been let loose upon us.

In most cases it is the simple, inevitable and direct, cause-and-effect result of our lack of faith, our fear and lack of trust in Him and the essential "rightness" of His universe. It is a reaction to the inner terror into which we relapse when *earthly* dangers and discomforts threaten.

There is no doubt that, if we took everything that happens to us as coming from God Who knows everything and *Who can do no wrong*—if we really *knew* "that all things work together for good in them that love God" (Rom: 8:28) then there would be a great lessening of illness among us—*even if there was no God!* How much more must it then be true where He does exist?

But we are men of little faith—and it is for faith that we must pray—not for being let off from the *results* of our lack of it.

Those who pray only for healing (and the comforting feeling that comes from having Him do it for us) may one day find that Jesus will say to them, "I never knew you: depart from me ye that work iniquity—seeking wonders that even Simon the Sorcerer could perform."

CHAPTER VI

The Nature of Faith

Having acquired at least a certain amount of insight into what is actually involved in "faith healing" and "miracles" (besides the unfortunate, emotional dramatics that usually surround this kind of thing), it is clear that the whole problem needs re-examination within the context of our beliefs.

Possibly first and foremost, the new question which here demands an answer is if we are now supposed to "put our trust" in medicines and doctors instead of in God?

Put like that it, as one can feel, almost intentionally distorts the issue. It is not a question of "putting one's trust" in medicines and doctors, and not in God. At the most one could admit that it is a matter of putting one's trust in a *certain* doctor, in the sense that one trusts that *he* is able, and willing, to apply all that the science of medicine can do for what ails us.

And again, it is wrong to say that in that case one "places one's trust" in the science of medicine for, what medicine does is no more than, to the best of its "human" abilities, to apply what it knows about the facts and forces of nature (that is: about the laws of God) for the purpose of correcting malfunctions and the aiding of the defensive systems of the living organism that is our body.

If we do not see it like that, we are still caught in the old pagan world-image that thinks of the world of matter (and the laws that rule it) as something that exists by itself, i.e.

a material world in and against which the metaphysical combination of our souls, aided by our God, have to wage a battle of survival!

There, when we fail, or do not know the answers, we turn to God Who is supposed to have greater powers and more knowledge about such things than we have—and we ask Him to save us if He can—or wants to.

This very definitely is not what our religion teaches us, although much that the church tells us seems to lead to this conclusion. Actually this idea is a contamination by the older religions among which ours grew into the form in which we know it now.

Among all of them, our religion (together with the Islam which branched off from the same stock) is the only one that knows only *one* God. And, of that God we believe that He created the "heavens and the earth" (which we now know to be the Universe in which the earth is only a relatively small speck of dust attendant on a minor star)—and everything that it contains. Unlike the other creation myths, in which there always is, either explicitly or implicitly, a pre-existing universe or environment in which the bringing forth or causing of the world and mankind takes place, *we* believe that everything, including the laws that rule it all, was brought into existence by what we call "God."

This "God," because of the limitations of our human imagination (which cannot think in terms other than those belonging to this earth) we visualise as "man-like" although only insofar as that we see Him as having the utmost perfection which it is possible for a mere human mind to imagine.

The truly religious who have finally left paganism behind, know that this is only a makeshift image. All of us accept that God is present everywhere, sees everything and hears everything or, to quote from Psalm 139: "Whither shall I go from thy spirit? or whither shall I flee from thy presence? If I ascend up to heaven, thou art there; if I make my bed in hell, behold thou art there. If I take the wings of the morning, and dwell in the uttermost parts of the seas; Even there shall thy hand lead me, and thy right hand shall hold me." And, as this must be true for every individual human being at all times of the day, and night, it can hardly be considered to be compatible with the image of a localised presence of a God sitting on His throne.

That God has a human shape, hair and hands and feet and everything that is implied in that, is also an essentially heathen idea which takes the text that God made us "in His image" as applying literally *to our bodies* and not to our souls and to the faintly flickering little nightlight of our "understanding."

The universe, that God originally created, "generated" (a term derived from that used in Gen. 2:4) man according to the latest possibilities He had placed in it and, at present, we find ourselves in a world in which everything is ruled by very definite laws. Everything happens according to those laws *and in no other way*.

It is in this world—and according to the laws that He made inherent in it, that we have to live as best we can in every physical aspect of our life.

It is also foolish to sit back and to wait for God to do a "miracle" for our special benefit.

We have been allowed to develop an intellect and we have been permitted to attain a measure of basic understanding of the physical conditions among which we live and in which our bodies form an essential part. We should learn to *use* these talents and woe to us if we "are afraid and hide that talent in the earth," like the bad servant in the parable. As we have been given a mind to think with, we should do so; and it is strange to find how often the Church seems to think it sinful if we do that in any other way than for the purpose of explaining the contradictions that are scattered throughout the text of the Bible. Only there the exercising of human ingenuity and inventiveness is not looked down upon with disdain.

It is a primitive and essentially pagan idea that God ordains plagues and sufferings for mankind and that it is wrong to do something about them, if it is at all possible.

These plagues and sufferings are no more than a part of the pattern of the universe that God created. They have not been *inserted* specially to punish or to try us. (In passing, it does not seem to have been realised that, in that case, even these plagues would have to be "miracles.")

There is nothing wrong in our using knowledge and our reasoning abilities for the purpose of overcoming them. There is no real difference between a farmer who uses his knowledge of when to plant his seeds, and at what time; and which of them is most likely to be the best for the given circumstances so that he will have the most favourable chance to reap a good harvest—and attempts to control rainfall or to use a vaccine against a plague.

In a similar way we should mobilise all our resources to discover methods of combating disease *and use the results*. Not to do so, but to ask God to do the healing, is to hold God's gifts in contempt.

At the same time, while doing everything we can to overcome the dangers of life, we should keep our human fears in check, in the steadfast knowledge that, even if we do not and *cannot* understand it, everything somehow happens as it should—even if that means pain and suffering, or death for us or those whom we love.

It is the combination of doing all that one can with the unshakeable conviction that, whatever happens, in the end it is part of a divine, and therefore perfect, pattern of events, which is the hall-mark of the true believer.

This however contains the basic idea that, *as far as the physical world is concerned*, we must depend upon our own efforts and not ask God to do anything special for us at all.

Once having created His universe and found it to be "good" (that is, "perfect") He cannot be asked, and even expected, to interfere on our behalf. If it was necessary for Him to interfere, that would, in itself, imply an imperfection in His original creation—and that is something that it is impossible to accept.

And, after all, what can *we* know about it? Is it not possible, for instance, that saving our life would endanger that of somebody else? And who are we to choose for God who is the more important in the overall pattern?

Knowing (as we believe that He does) everything, even the future, He would have known that the day would come when He would have to interfere, so why, being almighty, should He have let it come to such a pass?

Surely the thought that this could be possible is a symptom of bad faith.

Surely too, if what we fear is *not* necessary, it would have been included in the original design that it will not happen —and, therefore, however bleak the future may look to us now, it will not happen when the time comes.

On the other hand, if it does happen, *despite the utmost efforts from our side* (working within the pattern of His laws) that must be proof to us that it was necessary—and only a foolish mind would presume to criticise it on the basis of the grain of knowledge and understanding that he has.

How can we pretend to understand anything where an unbroken chain of cause and effect runs from the place where each created atom was at the beginning, billions of years ago, to the place where it is now?

What we need is faith and fortitude and a fitting respect for something that is so inconceivably immense that the imagination staggers and stumbles even after the first steps we try to take.

In two or three generations no one here will remember that our human mortal shape existed, so what does it matter in the annals of the universe if we are healthy or sick, rich or poor, successful or miserable failures? All we can do is to take God's world as it is and to live our life as best we can, trusting in Him while causing as little suffering as we can to others, hoping that they will do the same to us.

In *this physical life* we must look after ourselves according to the best of our ability, using whatever gifts we have been given, because they too are part of the pattern and should be used as such.

It is therefore (reverting to the question with which we started this chapter) not a question of "putting our trust" in medicine and doctors instead of in God, where it concerns the healing of our illnesses.

It is not a question of "trust" at all but of doing the best we can.

The trust should be in God. We must accept that *whatever* happens, it will be according to His will and design—something that cannot possibly be understood by us but that we *know* is as it should be.

CHAPTER VII

The Religion of the Child

Slowly the argument is penetrating to the nub of the problem.

Faith healing simply cannot be considered as a subject on its own. It is so intimately interwoven into the nature and quality of our religious conceptions that the one cannot be honestly examined without the other.

They cannot be separated into two topics of discussion and one can quite confidently say, "Tell me what you think of faith healing and I will tell you the quality of your belief in God."

If we really believe in a God Who is almighty and all-knowing—and have no doubt that *everything* happens according to His laws (and therefore never against His will), we have to realise that, in asking Him to heal us, we are not asking Him to help us *against* a disease.

We are having the presumption to ask Him that He SHOULD STOP MAKING US SICK!

If we ask Him to help us against disease, that is: "to be on our side," we demonstrate that our religion has not progressed beyond the one we learnt in Sunday school, the one that was based on seeing God as the "Father" who is a manifest extension and almost a generalisation of the flesh-and-blood father who ruled our home.

In those days, within the context of what was our family,

he was the man who loved us and was concerned about our well-being, but who punished us when we had transgressed against the rules that he had laid down. He was a tower of strength to whom we could turn for solace when we had been hurt and for help against the great, and often dangerous, "outside world."

Then, when in time, we grew up and went "outside" where we were on our own and had to look after ourselves, the God of our Sunday school took over our father's functions.

He too was concerned about our well-being, punished us when we transgressed against His laws and helped us against the "others" who—if we ever took the trouble to think about it—we considered to be, at best, no more than His step-children.

As St. Paul wrote to the Corinthians: "When I was a child, I spoke as a child, I understood as a child, I thought as a child; but when I became a man, I put away childish things."

We should grow up; but the process of growing up is not easy.

It is extremely difficult and often painful to "leave home" —and few of us dare to do it. We prefer to remain children, so that we keep on talking and understanding and thinking —and finally—acting like children.

This would not be so bad if we were really honest about it and admitted not only that we were children but that our thinking was childish too (or, should one put it more gently and call it "child-like"?).

This is, however, not at all as it is!

We are not merely rather unpleasant children who bicker and cheat and play each other dirty tricks. In life and the things of this life, we consider ourselves to be fully grown up! We think that our thoughts are valid—and only when we get into real trouble do we suddenly revert to the child-like state in which we ask "Father" to fix things up for us.

We try to have it both ways and there is little of the grown up man in us; the man who says: "I am the master of my fate. I am the captain of my soul. I take responsibility for what I do and if I drive my ship to founder on the rocks, I will not whimper."

In our wheedling prayers there is little of the spirit of the Man Jesus who said to God: "O my Father, if this cup may not pass away from me, except I drink it, thy will be done."

The "Father-image" of God is untenable in the *real* world in which we live.

Within the family, our father could hold the balance of justice reasonably true. The issues were never very grave, the number of personal interests were overseeable, and the common good over-rode most of the petty disputes. Even if our father did have a favourite amongst his brood, it did not really matter. Family life, was after all, a preparation for the life outside and *there* favouritism would certainly be something that the child-become-man would have to be able to live with.

What the Father-image religion has made out of our world, however, contains all the unpleasant aspects of family life and very little of the good. Instead of the universal brotherhood of man—with all of us helping one another against the inimical material world—and being helped and directed by God as the Father of this family—we see a wheedling for special favours, a jockeying for position, a flattering of God's Ego (as *we* think, judging Him by ourselves), a singing of hymns of praise (not because of true adoration but with an eye to being singled out for what could almost be called "promotion")—and all of this is often extended to the point where things are done "behind God's back" as if He could not see us there!

In this respect, our "childish" thinking eventually arrives at the point where it accepts that God only knows what men know and our public image is the one that we think that we must have in God's eyes. As long as we can hide our devious ways from other *men*, God will not know about them either —*just as it was in the family of our childhood.*

This is not only apparent in those "little" things that permit someone, who *really* considers himself to be a pious man, to be a crook—"but never on Sundays." The effect of the Father-image of God, combined with the childish thinking of mankind, can be seen in almost all of our less amiable characteristics.

It causes in us the reprehensible idea that, out of all the millions of men who are alive today—each one as unquestionably "human" as we are—God only really knows about us and those in our immediate environment (as if He were seeing the world through *our* eyes!). The others are merely there. Their relationship to God and God's relationship to them does not concern us. We refuse to think about it and its implications.

In war, especially, God becomes the God who "fights" on our side and Who helps to uphold the cause that is just for no other reason than that it is *our* cause.

It does not occur to us to ask whom or what He is "fighting" when He does this. At most, we think of it as "the forces of evil," not realising that, in doing so, we are readmitting the existence of other (albeit lesser) gods—the aftermath of the polytheism of our original ancestors.

Neither does it occur to us that the way in which He fights on our side is rather disappointing for One who is almighty so that, with even a minor effort, He (who created the whole Universe!) could undoubtedly make the "enemy" disappear as if they had never been.

The onlooker sees "the God of our fathers" fighting against "Die Gott unser Vatern" which is extremely foolish. Before the war He was both, but, because of *men* fighting each other, God is all at once supposed to have developed a split personality which is as self-destructive as idiot man himself!

It also does not help to rationalise the situation and to say that God does not fight as hard as He could do because the suffering of war is intended to "try" us.

As long as there is the idea that He "fights" at all, the image is distorted.

He does not "fight" but (conceding that He can and does interfere in His own creation) He can, at the most, be thought to adjust the ratio of suffering according to our respective deserts, *on both sides* of no man's land.

Although not so dramatically, this same thinking error is present in our daily life among ourselves, in our social and our economic relationships. God helps us *and therefore,* not our neighbour, not the competitor for our position in the office, not the client who is being bamboozled into paying too much for what he wants or needs—and not the "other side" that loses in an astute *but entirely lawful* business deal.

In thinking like this we simply *force* our common Father to take sides, not only in little things, but in matters that mean life or death, success or utter ruin.

We saw one of the more remarkable, if minor, examples of this when, not so long ago, a contender for the world heavyweight championship title prayed aloud for Victory—and, when he had won, proclaimed into the microphone that it was all due to God favouring him! One can understand what went on in the child-like mind of the fighter but, nevertheless, it remains a preposterous idea that He should be concerned with what bruiser-of-faces should be on top of the heap at any given moment.

We force God to take sides because, completely self-centred as we are, we forget that every victory entails a defeat. If we had remembered that, we would not merely pray for victory but at least try to find some reasonable cause for God to favour us but not the others—and if there were to be such a reasonable cause, how could we even dare to think that God would be unreasonable, and still permit us to be worsted?

In actual fact, we want God to make us win, or survive, or be successful *despite* any "reasons" there may be to the contrary—simply because we, to ourselves, are the most important people in the world.

If there are *real* reasons to expect that we will come out on top, it needs no great insight into human nature to know that we then will not appeal for His help. The businessman who has the market cornered and is entirely sure of what he is doing, does not ask God to help him take a fortune from the others. It is only when he is *not* sure that he will ask for divine assistance.

In all this, our presumption, face to face with an almighty God, is almost unbelievable! And this is as true of praying to be healed as it is of anything else.

What valid understanding can we possibly have of what we are really asking—of what would be entailed in granting us our prayer, even when asking God to "take sides" in our fight against a swarm of microscopic, non-human invaders?

How do we know if those invaders are not a necessary detail in the pattern of the whole? How do we know if, for instance, they are not being "trained" to wipe out half the population of the world in the fullness of God's own time?

And, if *that* is His design, who are we to criticise it? What can we know of the role that such a holocaust would have to play? (It is, in passing, a sobering insight into the way in which our childish mind works that it seems so much more ruthless to us that a few hundred million people should die at the same time, instead of, as they do now, individually and at more or less regularly spaced intervals!)

On the other hand, it is no less presumptive to twist one's "faith" to the extent of refusing to take what mundane, material measures against disease He has permitted us to discover, because "it would be wrong to interfere with the work of God."

Is it not, *must* it not be, that everything we do is a part of His plan? How could we possibly trip Him up? Even the mere thought that this could be possible is reducing God to the stature of a man—and not even a very superior man at that!

The first thing the person who is "growing up" should learn is that God, even if He has a fatherly interest *in all of us*, cannot be expected to "take sides"—even against the heathen, for they too must be His children, however "perverted" their conception of how He is.

Here too the egocentric nature of our typically childish

thinking comes to the surface. The idea (which seems to be inherent in the teachings of the different churches and sects) that only a certain creed, a certain way of approaching God and a certain conception of His nature can lead to what we call "salvation," is actually making God a member of that certain church or sect.

It is unblinkingly accepted that He can go counter to the laws He has laid down for nature—but he *has* to keep to those laid down by the "inspired" originator of the creed!

This strange twist is possibly the most markedly exemplified by the Roman Catholic belief that even God cannot grant salvation to a child that has died before it could be baptised.

The only textual justification for this rather primitive idea seems to be that St. Mark reports Jesus as saying: "He that believeth and is baptised shall be saved; but he that believeth not shall be damned."

Besides the fact that "not being baptised" is not specially mentioned as a cause for damnation (although it might lead to having to go through purgatory) the text, if used so literally, declares that *all* children that die below the age where they could possibly "believe," are eternally damned!

People who think like that do not seem to have read what God said to Moses (Ex. 33:19): "(I) will be gracious to whom I will be gracious, and will shew mercy on whom I will shew mercy," a text around which St. Paul built the ninth chapter of his Epistle to the Romans.

This insistence on special rites and special dialectical subtleties of belief as the only way to salvation (which, by implication and without the batting of an eye-lid, condemns most of mankind to perdition) clearly demonstrates the effect of the Father-image of God and the difficulty most so-called "true-believers" have in extending the family of which their God is the "Father," beyond their own parish—let alone to *all* humanity.

Yet, hypocritically, we hear it said, over and over again,

and by those same people, that all of us are children of One God!

Against this attitude Samuel already voices his disapproval in no uncertain terms.

"And Samuel said, Hath the Lord as great a delight in burnt offerings and sacrifices, as in obeying the voice of the Lord? Behold, to obey is better than sacrifice, and to hearken better than the fat of rams."

It is no use to hide behind the quibble that we no longer need to make sacrifices and burnt offerings. This statement applies as surely to "going to church on Sundays" and participating in the rites of our modern churches as it does to heathen "sacrifices."

One has to accept that even the pagan who *honestly* believes in and hearkens to *his* god will have a better chance of salvation than the "Sunday christian" with whom we are so distressingly familiar in our daily life that we almost take him for granted.

After all the pagan god is *not* "another god."

How (without making God party to a deception practised on His defenceless creatures) can one possibly believe otherwise than that the "god" of the pagans is how God Himself has made Himself manifest to them—in such a way that it would be possible *for them* to understand?

CHAPTER VIII

The Religion of the Adolescent

When it is time for the young man to leave his father's house, he does so equipped with the armoury he has taken over from his childhood environment. He now has a more or less complete set of values, concepts and the ideas that have been a self-evident part of his life. That was and still is how the world is. He has never known it to be seriously questioned nor has he felt the need to do so himself. Those values and principles have, for him, an *absolute* validity—basic and obvious as the law of gravity.

If he has a healthy self-confidence, he will go forth into the world and make himself a place in the society he finds there. Naturally he will have to make some adjustments as that society is not as closely integrated and mutually interdependent as his family was but, if he has been correctly educated, he will be able to make the necessary rectifications. In using his equipment and his values, he finds that, in his culture (built, as it is, on the same principles as those on which his home teaching were based) most of them remain fully operative. A few may have to be jettisoned because of the gradual change which takes place from generation to generation—and the rest with a bit of tinkering, will be found to be tolerably acceptable.

Besides that, one can always "compromise."

In doing this he learns, sooner or later, to fight his own battles, to justify and assert his own position in the community and to find his personal satisfaction both in "belonging" among his fellow men and in succeeding in what he wants to achieve. (That, in our modern, disintegrating culture, this has now often become impossible—or at least very difficult—to do is one of the main causes of the "opting out" of such a large number of our present crop of adolescents but that is because our culture is, itself, sick and dying at the roots. What has been said above applies to how it was and how the adolescent *should* still be, as he moves from childhood into maturity).

His parents, even if he is often not conscious of it, still remain the "home base," the anchorage and the rock on which his subjective world-image is founded. He turns back to them for comfort, advice, approval, consolation, encouragement and even help. Their authority and power over him have faded out but their disapproval hurts and their appreciation pleases so that trying to avoid the one and gaining the other still plays an important part in his life. But there is little more than that.

The religion of the adolescent (of those who do not outgrow this stage) has similar characteristics and in it God takes on a double personality. He is no longer only the "Father" but also—and mainly—the "King." This King has laid down the laws and determined the specific values with which the adolescent has grown up—and He rules according to those laws. As he sees it (as he *knows* it to be) it is the duty of every individual to live according to those laws and to respect those values. It is also one's privilege to be a living and active part of the glories of that kingdom.

Clearly this is also a satisfying religion. One knows what is "good" and what is "bad," not merely because "Father" has told us so but because it *is* so. Even God Himself has to obey those laws and judge according to those values. One can achieve things and be appreciated for achieving them. One has a standard by which to appraise the value of others and of oneself. Above all, there being only one God (whose Kingdom is not really threatened by the machinations of a revolutionary Satan) one is safe as long as one keeps within the laws and sure of an ultimate award, which is guaranteed by the state exchequer.

And the paternal avatar of God is also still there because —as a son of the King—there is still the possibility of retaining exactly as much of the "God the Father" image as one needs for more personal and emotional purposes. There is still Someone to Whom one can go for advice, encouragement and personal sympathy and, again, help—*because, after all, one is a better and more loyal son than the others!*

At the same time, as was shown during the rise of Islam and the conquering of the world by the West (especially the deeds of the Spaniards in Middle America) this "adolescent mode" of religion (like the state, and the chauvinism it induces), has some most unpleasant and dangerous possibilities.

When one knows how it should be and how people should act, one need not be content with living like that. One can also tell, and even try to force, others to do it too. One can even make that one's calling and be ready and willing to sacrifice everything, including one's life, in following it.

For the Islamic explosion with its overt battle cry of "Kill the Infidels" this was at least an honest effort towards eliminating everyone who did not hold himself subject to the only legitimate "King," but with the Spaniards in Mexico and Peru another factor becomes evident which, even if it is no more than "human," is one that mars the purity of this sort of fanatical, interfering type of religion. The "incidental" personal advantages to be gained from confiscating the possessions of those "punished" for their "sins" can easily become the real incentive when one can please one's God and enrich oneself in the bargain.

The protracted religious wars that racked the Middle Ages, the Crusades zealotry, witch hunting and aggressive bigotry in general were and are all products of the same attitude of mind, an attitude which *sanctifies* the interference with the life of others while, in a more gentle but no less persuasive mood, our missionaries belong there too.

If one *knows* what people should do it is difficult not to tell them about it or to remain silent when they seem to get away with what one has to stop oneself from doing.

In our day a new and very interesting development has made its appearance as people no longer see the religious aspects of life as the "Kingdom of God" but as a republic of which God as become the president. It is no longer ruled by immutable, eternal laws but by laws that adjust themselves to the thinking and the wishes of men.

In this context the theologue sees an "improvement" in the God-image during the ages because, as man developed, he gradually "purified" his original "primitive" concept of God, thereby making it less "earthy" and (therefore?) more "true." God may, in this way, even come to "abhor" the disenfranchisment of minorities (or even majorities) because He is, at heart, a true Democrat.

But even then the adolescent, for himself, never loses his primary characteristic, namely that he never examines his basic premises—those that he *knows* to be so.

To him it is simply inconceivable and it does not even enter his mind (other than with a brimstone smell of blasphemy) that his "basic facts" could be invalid.

Contradictions in his creed he either does not see, or refuses to see, or simply refers to the "Eternal Mystery" of God for solution. He *knows* that, whatever God's reasons and purposes, they will not contradict or clash with what he himself knows to be right. *That* at least cannot be wrong and it is up to God to solve the riddles that his creed may produce when it is put into practice.

Lastly, because the laws which define his "good" and "bad" are given in his scriptures, there is (as in the human state and its law courts) the possibility for interpreting them to suit one's particular needs and tastes. To mention but a few out of our own religion, we have the abolishment of several clearly stated death sentences, the passing over of the prohibition of divorce and the injunction not to spare the rod for fear of spoiling the child.

The adolescent, in the goodness of his heart, knows that God could not "really" have meant that; and what *he* knows is true.

Thus, as can be seen, even the religion of the adolescent is an altogether convenient and comfortable religion to have.

CHAPTER IX

The Religion of the Adult

Here and there among men there is an individual who does not close his eyes to the contradictions he finds in his religion; a man to whom the questioning of, and wanting to know more about it, is not a sin while, "That is something only God can know," is not an acceptable answer until a full and honest attempt has been made to find a better one.

It is obviously not honest to make or accept a set of rules and laws and premises to suit one's personal ideas of how it should be and then, when these lead to incongruities, to shrug one's shoulders while maintaining that, nevertheless, those laws and premises remain valid. Therefore, the man who is finally growing up does not hold on blindly to all he has absorbed holus-bolus from the environment of his youth. He gathers up his forces and, closing his eyes in what is almost a prayer for guidance, joins battle with what, for him, has become unacceptable.

The God of nearly all religions is, recognizably, "human" —He is, at the very least, definitely seen as a "person."

He is "conscious," He knows what He is "doing" and he always has some "reason" for whatever He does. He has a "past" that cannot be changed (even by Himself) and a future in which, what He does now, is *"intended"* to lead to a specific "result." He is, therefore, definitely subject to a Time in which He is irrevocably tied down to the present moment of his existing. Our God, to us, has, like us, a yesterday and a tomorrow.

What is more important here is that He also has individual "personal" qualities in that He is "loving," "perfect" and "just," "merciful," "all-knowing" and "all-understanding" even if the Old Testamentary quality of "jealousy" has lately been dropped because, being the only God, he can hardly have any other gods to be jealous of. (Besides that, "jealousy" has become a "bad" characteristic in our days of "live and let live" and "equal opportunities for everyone.")

The old fashioned quality which made Him into Someone to be "feared" obviously stems from the bad old days when it still was a "virtue" of Kings that they should be feared because that testified to their temporal power. Nowadays some of the "sports" which our religion has produced seem to be almost ready to pat Him on the back!

All these attributes are definitely *human* qualities and even a superficial examination shows that they cannot be the qualities of a God, *unless He is also "human"* albeit, shall we say, in a "higher" class. In a God they would contradict each other out of existence.

There would, for instance, be an unavoidable mutual exclusion between a divine, absolute "Justice" and an equally divine, absolute "Mercy."

It is manifestly wrong to think of a God who is "merciful to whom He is merciful" (and Who pays the late-coming sluggard the same wages as He pays to the worker who has conscientiously done his duty all day long) as a "Just" God. He may be "justified" in what He does for reasons of His own but He is not "just" in any sense that we give to that word.

And should one not be shocked (accepting that *all* men are God's creatures) at the blatant "injustice" of the Israelite God when He made Himself a partner in putting the inoffensive, peaceful inhabitants of Canaan to the sword?

This thinking error about the justice of God can be understood. We are so used to a human "justice" which can be tempered with mercy without becoming unjust (because the measure of guilt is never known or even definable while the amount of punishment is not clearly laid down so that it can, legally, vary between wide limits), that it seems permissible to think that there can also be a divine Absolute Justice which can be Merciful.

What has not been noticed here is that a divine Absolute Justice *cannot* be subject to *any* arbitrary variation in the scale of retribution or awards. *Where all the factors are known* (as they must be to an all-knowing God Who can look into the innermost chambers of our mind), they can add up to only one "just" answer. In whatever way one sees it, *any* mercy shown by God to a sinner is an injustice to all those who had to undergo full and deserved punishment. No matter what His reasons are, such "mercy" could not be anything else than "unjust."

Realising this, the adult thinker finds it necessary to delete either "Justice" or "Mercy," or both, from his list of the attributes of his God. He humbly replaces them by saying, and thinking, and *believing* that God does what He does and that, being "God," what He does is "good." He has to admit that he does not understand God's ways but, being human, that is also what he should already have admitted from the beginning and, slowly, he comes to realise *that* too.

Both "justice" and "mercy" are human qualities which, for us, do not contradict each other because we are blind and grope about in the dark for the meaning of what we do. As it is, we have no clear idea of what "guilt" is and know still less what the aim and object of "punishment" should be.

But that is not the end of the thinker's troubles.

If God is Omniscient and Almighty, it, logically, becomes almost impossible that there could have been anything He wanted to "achieve" with His creation or, in other words, that He could not have had any "purpose" with it.

This follows immediately from the fact that, being Almighty and knowing everything, He could have created it all as it was intended to be. Secondly, being the only God, there cannot be something like a malignant "Fate" or a blind "Chance" that could cross His way and frustrate His intentions.

If there had been anything that had to be achieved, if some "purpose" had to be attained, it seems to be a futile idea that God should have started His creation as somewhat different from what it had to be for the sole purpose of letting it "develop" towards a—merely possible (!)—ideal at the cost of an amount of human (and animal!) suffering that cannot even begin to be imagined. Yet, if the outcome was more than a "mere possibility" there would have been no "achievement of a purpose."

Finally, knowing the future, knowing what was (inevitably) going to happen, God's "observing" of the "development" of His creation must be something like going to see a film for a second time.

The difficulty here is that Omniscience and Omnipotence are not compatible with being bound to time. *Being bound to time is a characteristic of what has been created but it can hardly be a quality of the Creator unless that Creator Himself, has, also been created.*

If God, although bound by time, was Omniscient, He could either not know the future which does not yet exist (because it is not there to know) or know it as an *inevitable* development of what is in the present—which would mean that He either was not Omniscient or that, having created the universe He could go home because He knew exactly how it would all work out. He could also not be bound to time and be Omnipotent because, in that case, He would not be able to change the past.

In this way one could underline several more internal contradictions and logical impossibilities but these will have to suffice. They all demonstrate the same fact that rational thinking always has to come to the finding of an "Eternal Mystery"—the "Ultimate Riddle" that cannot be solved—the place where mere man has to throw up his hands and say, "Only God can know—I have to be content to leave it to Him."

This would naturally be the right attitude to take but only if it had prevented that same man from thinking that he still really knows quite a lot about it all.

What the careful, adult thinker realises here is that the fancied "mystery" has actually been created by himself and that, although his reasoning may have been absolutely correct, the substance and material with which he has reasoned is actually a collection of ideas and preconceptions in which a certain *expected* solution *has already been incorporated beforehand*. What actually constitutes the "mystery" is that the solution refuses to come out again!

He has found that it was not a matter of there being no answer but that there was no valid question.

What he has taken to the self-evident is that God *is* Omniscient, Omnipotent and Absolutely Just, Merciful, Loving and Perfect.

All these are beautiful, understandable and very human ideas—but they are not axiomata. They are not even "logical propositions" but, at best, tentative proposals (expressing the hope) that there should be Someone, higher and more permanent and powerful than the known earthly father and King, Someone Who, nevertheless, has kept the approachableness of the former and the might of the latter while retaining all that man recognises as "good" in himself— magnified into a state of absolute perfection.

That there is such a Someone is not a statement of fact. *Even if that idea,* to a greater ar lesser degree, *is present in all men,* that does not make it into a "truth." *All men* also believe that the sun comes up in the East and goes down in the West and that idea has remained so even after most of them have learnt to accept that the piece of earth on which they live turns and tilts towards and away from the sun as the earth rotates in space. Or tell a man that a great plain is "not flat" and he will look at you in unbelief (until he realises that you mean that it bulges up in the middle—like a portion of the surface of a sphere).

What we experience directly are "facts" to us. What we "know" to be the truth belongs to some other, more or less theoretical sphere of thinking which is not a part of our daily life.

When, therefore, considering the perfection of God, man finds that the idea leads to impossibilities and internal contradiction, he does not conclude that his premises are wrong. He does not even say, as the philosophers do, that he has found a "paradox." He raises his hands in a sign of surrender and says "This is an Eternal Mystery—something that only God Himself can understand."

From his side the adult thinker also comes to the conclusion that it is God *Himself* that is the Mystery and that all his own thinking has been no more than the to be expected failure of a piteous attempt at understanding Him in terms of human values and relationships.

But here, unlike the adolescent, he does not close his eyes and refuse to look.

He demands to know the truth, even if it kills him or threatens to wash all meaning out of life and eternity. Better that than to know, or to fear, that one is deluding oneself by means of a set of inspiring, but essentially invalid, images.

It is then, when he has almost given up all hope, that he realises that he has, at last, arrived at the Truth itself.

As said, our ideas about the qualities of God are merely idealisations of what we recognise as "good" in ourselves—but that "good" is actually contingent on our being human—on the *possibility* of our being "bad."

Where it is impossible to be otherwise, "virtue" is no longer a virtue. The asexual man is not "chaste" when he does not indulge in the pleasures of the flesh nor can be a saint unless he has battled to subdue his sinful tendencies. In the same way God cannot be "good" if He does not have the potential to be "bad" yet, such is the internal contradiction of our human thinking, we cannot think of something as being "absolutely good" if it has retained the possibility of being bad.

Therefore, what the really religious, adult person should school himself to do is *to stop himself from trying to understand God in terms of human values.*

He must teach himself to accept that God is, *in all respects,* a Mystery. He should even stop thinking about Him as "Him"—as was so cleverly underlined by the Women's Lib Ms. who said that she certainly believed in God—she had believed in Her all her life. To avoid the male pronoun we have to invent a special one for God because the word "It" has too strong an association with material "things." Let us, in future, use the totally capitalised form of "IT."

What is interesting here is that our thinker has finally arrived at the starting point of almost all religions. God has to be the "Eternal Mystery" *to us.*

The point is that IT should *remain* that Eternal Mystery.

We can know nothing about God, not because IT *is* mysterious but because *we* can only think in earth- and time-bound thoughts. Our virtues—with which we think to "adorn" IT—are virtues *only* for us. They are virtues only in the circumstances and conditions in which *we* find ourselves.

We should use them as they are intended to be used—to perfect our *own* life here on earth—*they have no other meaning.*

CHAPTER X

Man and the Mystery

All our creeds and churches and sects (as a matter of fact all of man's religions) begin with the presence of a central "Divine Mystery" and yet all of them follow up this basic declaration of faith by telling us about how He is and what He does—and even "why"—sometimes into almost preposterous details. In doing this, they seem to be completely unaware of the primary truth that it must be a blasphemous impudence to claim that, even if God is the Ultimate and Ineffable Mystery, He *also* is thus and so and that.

Can the ant understand the music of the stars or the earthworm know the reason for the rain that wets the mulch in which it lives?

This "humanising" of God is, however, an almost necessary quality of all public, organised church or temple religions. They cannot do without it—but that is also the central hub of their dilemma. How *far* can one go in claiming to know the mysteries of God?

As one does not know everything, one has to admit the existence of a Mystery but, at the same time, to be a viable religion that can support its temples and its hierarchy of priests or preachers, it has to teach something that can be known about God.

One should not overlook that the Christian churches are in active and often vicious competition with each other so that they have taken over the "jealousy" of God (in relation to other Christian Gods?) and made it their own where it concerns their members. Although they all believe in the same God and have the same scriptures to go by, their individual existence depends upon some special interpretation of a detail of the word of God—and they must continually hammer that home.

Proclaiming a God Who is really a total and complete eternal Mystery would fill few benches in a church!

Even the God Who says: "I do what I will!" although he is manifestly not a "just" God, is at least a divine Person—and with a "person" one can argue and wheedle and successfully curry favour. A church and a priesthood can make a living out of that.

The defining and preaching of a God *with certain* characteristics lessens the Mystery and, inevitably, it will *be found that the active life of the church turns round the aspects of Him that are no longer a part of the Mystery*. Thus the Mystery is pushed away into the background as far as it will go.

As we know, there is no limit to theorising except the innate credulity of the audience and it is, therefore, inevitable that, very soon religions will appear that *know* everything—or at least almost everything—about what God does, what He likes and what He abhors.

Then, when something happens that an "ideal" man (that is: God as imagined and defined) would not have allowed to happen, one is referred to the Universal Standby, to the Eternal and Unknowable Mystery of God. In effect the church says: "Only God knows why, in this case, He should have done something that goes against the characteristics *I* have given Him. We will only be able to understand it in the hereafter."

The adult mind simply does not accept this way of thinking once its essential fallacy has been realised.

The man gathers his strength and all the fortitude he can muster to learn to live with an Ineffable Mystery the application to which the ideal values of mankind do not even begin to make sense—a Mystery that may not even know that he exists but of which he has to believe that whatever happens through IT has to be as it has to be. He cannot even give himself the pleasure of thinking that what happens must be "good."

But, it will be said, if one thus "dehumanises" God, one dissolves the very foundations from under all our moral and ethical convictions.

To a man who can believe in this depersonalised Mystery, the laws of God and the teachings of the Bible will be a mere wind of words. His conscience, if he ever had one, will atrophy and he will be able to commit the most disgusting atrocities without a qualm.

One could never trust a man like that!

It is, however, a rather humbling fact that the truth is exactly the opposite!

In the first place it will be found that by far the largest part of the atrocities that we can remember were inflicted on fellow men in the name of, or to the glory of, some God. Was it not the main sop to our consciences, when we set out to conquer the world by fire and sword, that we were called up to convert it to Christianity?

And, among ourselves, what of the "Auto da Fe's," what of what the Spaniards did to the Dutch during the Eighty Years war, and the slaughter of the Huguenots in Paris and the Camisards in the Cevennes—and did not Calvin, who is the father of many Protestant creeds, have his opponent in the matter of the tenets of predestination and election, arraigned for blasphemy, condemned and burnt to death?

One closes one's eyes in disgust at the record of the practical results of our belief in a gentle Jesus Who taught us to turn the other cheek.

On the other hand, it is to say the least, extremely unlikely that an atheist would torture a believer in order to convert him to Atheism!

It is what we believe that we *know* about God and His works that allows us to interfere in the lives of others and to justify the use of brutalities on those who do not conform—but it does not keep *us* from sinning! God's punishment (if He punishes at all?) is not immediate enough to hold us in leash. Hence we find that the Church has to call in the help of a policeman to stop us, at least from sinning in public by Sunday closing laws for bars and swimming baths and public games and theatres—not to mention anti-gambling laws and others such.

In actual fact, the idea that the dehumanising of God must lead to a breakdown of moral and ethical standards of behaviour in a man, is the product of "childish" or "adolescent" thinking.

The childlike person is "good" because he fears punishment by the Father, or desires His goodwill or love. The adolescent is "good" because he is convinced that one should obey the law.

Neither of these is good because that is how *he* is.

Both are under constraint.

Both are good because they have to be—or else! And both therefore imagine that, if that constraint is removed or even relaxed (because the Father has become something strange and incomprehensible and the laws of God have become meaningless *as such*) that the natural evil in the man will take the upper hand (as, in the secret chambers of their hearts they may often have dreamed about).

But what "good" is there in something that is merely "not evil"?

Evil not done for fear of punishment, or good done in hope of reward, is not in the man, but in the law and in the ability of the lawmaker to punish or to reward. Without the latter the former would not have been. Evil would, and good would not have been done.

Fear of punishment and hope for reward are not a *virtue* in man! He has that trait in common with even the most primitive of animals. A dog can learn not to chew the carpet and to sit up and beg, and rats—and even fishes—yes, even planarian worms have been taught similar things.

Must we therefore consider the virtue of man to be no more than that? Truly, for a man to be virtuous, that virtue must reside in, and come out of himself—it must be an integral part of him!

It is true that, if one takes away the father *from the child* it will go on a rampage, doing all the things it has never been allowed to do. If one jerks the foundations from under the laws *of the adolescent,* he will be lost and unable to resist his inclinations that they have held in check for him up to now.

And as man always judges others by himself—he thinks that it will be the same with the adult.

But this is not necessarily true, for it must not be forgotten that, although the child is a child because it is one, and the adolescent is an adolescent because that is his nature, the grown-up is grown up because he *has* grown up. The process of growing up does not mean the throwing overboard of all the comforting and consoling *and* restraining influences of earlier beliefs—it is an essential revaluation of them.

If the jettisoning of irritating restraints had been the intention, there would have been the simple turning to Atheism or Agnosticism. Replacing God the Father, by God the Lord Almighty and then by the Eternal Mystery, which is finally and humbly acknowledged as above and beyond all human understanding, shows an entirely different train of mind.

The changing of God the Father to the Lord Almighty is not a diminishing of His stature—rather the reverse. And so it is with the next step from the Lord Almighty to the Ineffable Mystery.

In the same way, being good because of fear of punishment or hope of reward is lower than being good because of respect for the law. In the former the values are in relation to the self, in the latter they are in relation to a God-ruled Universe in which the individual desires to be worthy of his place.

When the adult has truly learnt to live and humbly to accept the Eternal Mystery as the background of his life, "good" and "evil," as such, lose their meaning. They are parochial concepts—but, for him, all values, reasons and ultimate purposes are somehow in that great Mystery.

The child lives in a world in which there are lots of things it would like to do but which it daren't, lots of things which it would like to have but which it is not allowed to touch. Its understanding goes no further and its life is concentrated on getting as much as it can, either by special permission, or by snatching when it thinks no one is looking.

As a matter of fact, it is this wall of prohibition around it that makes the forbidden things specially desirable to it.

The adolescent lives in a well ordered world, ruled by an enlightened and just power—and he tries to live with it as best he can—finding his satisfaction in being a worthwhile and, if possible, a significant part of it.

To the adult, however, there are no values worth mentioning in *this* world—certainly no external ones.

Neither power nor riches can have anything more than a local and temporary significance when the created world is seen in relation to the inconceivable beyond. Ambitions in those directions therefore look to him like the frenetic striving of a frog to be Lord Muck in its own puddle.

Being human, he may, time and again feel the urge to compete, or feel a twinge of loss at a chance that has been allowed to slip away. But, (as was already clear to the adult Solomon) his reason, if not his heart, tells him that it is all a "weariness of the flesh."

"Lay not up for yourselves treasures upon earth, where moth and rust doth corrupt, and where thieves break through and steal," is, for him not just a bit of beautiful but slightly unrealistic idealism, but a somewhat depressing, yet self-evident, truth. He knows that "you can't take it with you" and that, even if you could, what use would it be? Whatever it is that one treasures, it can only have its values *here*.

Moreover, he knows that the only meaning of the word "value" here below is the use one can have out of a thing *here*. It does not lie in the having of it, as is so clearly demonstrated, for instance by the various stratagems that owners of magnificent collections of fantastically "valuable" paintings or bric a brac have to employ to obtain at least *some* of that value out of them. One soon gets bored with wandering through room after room filled with precious objects—or showing them to "friends" in order to read the value of what one possesses in their envious eyes!

After all, one can live in but one house at a time, sleep in one bed and eat one breakfast, one lunch and one dinner a day—*if* one's digestion has not been ruined by earning them!

And what is honour and glory among men where the whole world is one big graveyard of those whose praises are no longer sung because even their names have been forgotten?

I do not know who and what my grandfather was and I know also that my grandchildren will only remember me as a vague image of an old man sitting at his desk in a booklined study. It is unlikely that they will transmit that little memory to their children.

But even if my name were to resound to the end of created time, like that of Socrates or Hammurabi—what would there be of *me* in the sounding of that name?

No—when all his values have their roots in the *Incomprehensible* Beyond, the "adult" is hardly likely to turn to crime, or to lose his moral balance, in a created world of physical reality which has no intrinsic value of itself.

CHAPTER XI

Faith and Healing

The religion (if it can be called a "religion") of the adult mind is a personal religion. It does not lend itself to embellishment by rituals or strengthening by communal worship. It cannot even be taught as it has to be personally and painstakingly wrested away from wishful thinking in the face of childish fears, an instinctive sense of blasphemy and the ever looming "cosmic terror" of the loner in an immense, impersonal (actually "lifeless") Universe.

The only form of "prayer" that makes any sense in it is something like the "quiet time" which plays such an important (and effective!) part in many of our sectarian religions and (in the form of "vigils") in most of the more "primitive" beliefs.

Above all, it needs the continuous enforcement of a developing "Faith" (a better word here would have been "Trust") —an inner confidence and conviction that, even if one cannot possibly understand *anything* (because such an understanding would have to be compounded of what can, at the best, be no more than translated manifestations of a few aspects of the whole of the Mystery), it *must* be as it *is* and, therefore, (translated into our earthly language) "Good."

It is towards the attainment of this state of mind that the "quiet time" is directed—towards a feeling of being in some mysterious way, a part of and, therefore "one" with the Mystery. This should then lead, not to a humble submission or a tearful self-abasement, but to an active *agreement* (which, being only human, need not necessarily be enthusiastic.)

Manifestly this is not a religion that can develop into a "church." It is exclusively concerned with the relationship between the individual and his God—the state of mind that Jesus intended when He told us to go into our room and shut the door behind us when we pray.

As such, this "prayer," this "quiet time" can also not be a routine ritual in one's life. It subserves its function only when the need for the easy solution of a divine "Father" or "King" becomes too strong or when the vicissitudes of life make it difficult for a mere human being to "agree" with what is happening.

On the other hand, this "religion" does away with neither the laws and rules of conduct, nor the knowledge of "good" and "bad," nor does it abolish mundane values. It rather perfects and actually strengthens them individually because it takes away the false, imaginary, "eternal rewards" and "eternal punishments" that, in practice, confuse and devaluate them by the promise of what the irreverent have come to call "pie in the sky" and the restraining of people only by the measure up to which they believe in and fear the threatened punishment in the hereafter.

The rules and laws and values that govern our lives have, in this view, become just that. *They are nothing more than that.* They are not anchored in an eternal background, the imagined nature of which can be tampered with by the fertile and ingenious mind of man in order to justify actions that can do untold harm to others while they are to the advantage of those who indulge in such distortions—or give certain groups of people the right to interfere in the lives of others.

If we avoid this kind of thinking, "good" becomes its own "award" which lies in being aware of doing and having done the "right" thing. The deed has actually, not been "good," it has been "correct."

"Sin" also becomes its own punishment which lies in knowing that one has lowered one's standards and, therefore, oneself—in the realisation that one has "failed," i.e. a loss of self-respect. (That this "punishment" is something the nature of which can, nowadays, hardly be understood, so that many would smile at the idea that it *is* a punishment, does not matter here. It works on the "faith" of the adult).

The rules themselves are essentially very simple. They are "honesty"—especially being honest *with oneself*—and not doing *avoidable* harm to others.

Naturally this is not even the material out of which an ethical system can be built up in practice! It is, and must remain, a private creed as no one but oneself can judge how "honest" one has been; how honestly one has weighed the value of that to which one knows oneself to have a "right" against that which one has done to "earn" it. Still less is it possible for others to know or judge how honestly one has weighed the disadvantages (and even harm) one has thought it right to cause others against the scale of what was actually "avoidable."

The rules and laws and values that apply in any given instance have no eternal, absolute or other external backing or foundation. They are what defines the structure and pattern of a certain society, culture or other grouping among men and must, for that reason—and only for that reason—be faithfully and willingly obeyed. They are different for different people and gradually change with the nature of those actions and relationships they rule but this makes no difference to their validity and the adult conforms to the best of his ability (like everyone should), not for hope of reward or fear of punishment (temporal or eternal) but because that is how his social context *is*.

As said, this cannot be anything else than a personal creed and, as few people who are at all concerned about such things can live without some form of a "God the Father" or a "God the King" (even if these may, nowadays have become overtly political) that alone makes any attempt at proselytising a foregone failure.

Man, being what he is, the organised religions, churches, sects, splinter religions, swamis and other cults are an essential part of the human scene. Men could not live without them and, hence, they perform a necessary task. A breakdown here (like the one which seems to be threatening now) would result in a chaos worse than that which has come on the world after the breakdown of the Pax Britannica in the first half of this century.

Where the latter has left us a gabble of larger and smaller states warring with whatever weapons they can find, a breakdown of religion would leave most individual men rudderless in a world they no longer could understand.

In the deepening gloom of the end of what we have known as our "civilisation" the creed of the adult enables him to preserve at least a small area where what he does makes sense. It also enables him to take what steps he can to give himself a chance of survival as it, very definitely, is not the religion of the meek, a suicide or a passive resister. It is the religion of a participator.

The need to survive (to say that this is a "right" is mere linguistic pomposity) is an integral part of the structure of the manifestation of the Eternal Mystery in which we live and it would be foolish to think that one knows better than God how it "should" be.

All that one can know with a certain amount of confidence is what, in any given case, one *oneself* should do or leave undone. It is futile to presume to judge the deeds of others in any other way than that laid down by the official laws covering the circumstances.

When, after what has been discussed, we now take a second look at the problem of Faith Healing, it turns out to be only a part—a relatively small part—of our attitude to God, to Life and to reality.

Basically it is the question of if one should expect God, or whatever one acknowledges as the Supreme Power, to interfere on *our* behalf in the smooth running of His own creation and at *our* request.

This does not only include sickness and health, or winning at games of chance and similar lesser issues, but success and failure in business, love, parenthood, life and death —in short, in all the weal and woe and all the numerous vicissitudes of our life.

Seen in the context of the whole, it is futile to expect God to interfere.

This would overlook or deny the fact that all life is competition and that (at least in every situation where the help of the Supreme Power is requested or needed) helping a particular individual means that that Supreme Power must "take sides" against another.

Even in curing a disease, in deferring the moment of death, all those who would have benefited from that death, all those who could have taken over the employment, earned the money, eaten the food, loved the husband or wife, taken his seat in the bus or in the "full" theatre, would be proportionately prejudiced and suffer the proportionate loss because the Power had seen fit to decide that the man should get better, the woman survive or the child live on.

The idea, that a Power, or any Divine Entity, should or could, or would do this obviously stems from a distorted view of the whole. It is based upon the preconception that one's own person and well-being has more importance than that of others, not only to oneself but to the whole of the Universe—which must be influenced by *any* "miracle."

This megalomania is understandable but manifestly foolish if one gives it but a moment's thought. It is the result of, like a child, seeing only the personal environment—and even that only (and almost self-evidently) from one's own standpoint.

It actually implies that the MYSTERY is a God who sees the world through *our* eyes, with *our* valuations and *our* judgments—which is a thoroughly primitive and heathen attitude, grown out of the days when every man had his own god and all households their own lares and penates.

The first thing that the thinking person should learn to acknowledge and accept is therefore that, in the world of reality, all things happen as they must and that one can only influence them by being a "cause" that will have an "effect," according to the way in which things work.

We have developed a brain that can understand at least part of how things work. We have a body that can, at our behest, do things and make things—and we should use those gifts to the utmost of their potentials—both in the "competition" of life among others and in the fight against disease. We must develop our understanding to the maximum in order to defend our body against invaders. We should try to repair it where the inherent repairing mechanisms fail—and give it the best possible environment we can while abusing its recuperative powers as little as we can manage.

In all this there is no externally imposed limit, no divine barrier beyond which we dare not look. The limit lies *in us,* in the limit that there is to our understanding—and even that limit is less narrow than we tend to think.

When, however, we have done all that we can, there comes a time when we can do no more and have to leave the issue to "fate"—or to God—to decide.

It is then that the moral testing comes, for even then there is really no "deciding" as we think. Things will still happen as they must, determined by factors over which we have no control.

And, although we may believe in a God who could have the power to determine the outcome, He would have to do that by *creating* forces or new points of existing by a miracle, to help us, if the outcome written in the situation had originally been adverse.

Who are we to ask for all this? How, within the realms of the reasonable can we expect that, to prevent *us* temporary grief, God should cause the sun to stand still (for the size of the miracle could hardly be important to a Supreme Power!) ?

And the irony of all this is that, once the miracle has been done, once we are better, or the child has been "brought back from the grave," we will risk our life and that of the child by breaking the speed limit, by wildly overtaking other cars, so that we can get a somewhat better position for ourselves in the drive-in!

We do not even seem to realise that if, as we have implied by our prayers, God were to be a "Person" with some Personal pride, all we should expect from Him is that He will blot us out against a tree and have done with us!

The only honest attitude, *when we have done all we can*, is to say, in the weakness of our human hearts, "If it be possible, let this cup pass from me,"—although we know very well that what will happen is the *only thing possible*.